LIFE'S LITTLE TREASURE BOOK

TREASURE BOOK

On Love

H. JACKSON BROWN, JR.

RUTLEDGE HILL PRESS

NASHVILLE, TENNESSEE

Published in Nashville, Tennessee, by
Rutledge Hill Press, Inc., 211 Seventh
Avenue North, Nashville, Tennessee 37219.
Distributed in Canada by H. B. Fenn and
Company Ltd., Mississauga, Ontario.

Typography by D&T/Bailey Typesetting, Inc.,
Nashville, Tennessee
Illustrations by Greg King
Floral art by Cristine Mortensen
Book design by Harriette Bateman

ISBN: 1-55853-329-X

Printed in Hong Kong through Palace Press
2 3 4 5 6 7 8 9 — 99 98 97 96

INTRODUCTION

$\mathcal{I}$magine a world without love and romance. No love poems or love letters. No Romeo and Juliet. No Sir Lancelot and Guinevere. No Clark and Lois. No Mickey and Minnie. No heart-shaped boxes of chocolates or long-stemmed roses that say, "I'll love you forever." No heights of passion or depths of despair.

In love, we are at our best and our silliest. In love, we are the only two people on the planet, certain that no others have felt the same way we do.

Love can come at a first glance across a crowded room or it can creep up on us, growing slowly like the tendrils of a morning glory vine until it suddenly bursts into flower one sunny day.

Love has many faces. Young love is wild and outrageous, laughing at moderation and blinding us to common sense. Mature love is composed and sustaining; a celebration of commitment, companionship, and trust. It is the lucky man and woman who experiences both.

The poet John Dryden called love "a noble madness." To Cole Porter, it was "that old black magic." The Beatles convinced us that "all you need is love." As the entries in this book reveal, love is all that and much, much more.

❧

$\mathcal{L}$ove is when the
other person's
happiness is
more important
than your own.

*L*ove is like wildflowers.
It's often found in the most
unlikely places.

❧

*Treasure the love you
receive above all.
It will survive long after
your gold and good health
have vanished.*

—Og Mandino

*B*e patient.

❧

*B*e kind.

❧

*B*e faithful.

Buy a box of children's valentines and hide them around the house for your sweetheart to find throughout the year.

❧

Love consists in this,

that two solitudes protect and

touch and greet each other.

—Rainer Maria Rilke

To love someone

is to see a miracle

invisible to others.

—François Mauriac

❦

At the touch of love
everyone becomes a poet.

—Plato

$\mathcal{B}$elieve in love at first sight.

❧

$\mathcal{N}$ever stop the wooing.

❧

$\mathcal{W}$hen picking up your sweetheart at the airport, be waiting at the gate with a bouquet of balloons or flowers.

$\mathscr{I}$'ve learned that . . .

you're never too old to be
bitten by the love bug.

—Age 81

a homemade banana cream
pie will impress a man
more than a new dress and
a new hairdo.   —Age 44

Take long, hand-holding moonlit walks.

❧

Don't eat onions unless she does.

❧

Don't let her drive on slick tires.

How do I love thee?
Let me count the ways.
I love thee to the depth and
breadth and height
My soul can reach. . . .
I love thee with the breath,
Smiles, tears, of all my life!
—and, if God choose,
I shall but love thee better
after death.

—Elizabeth Barrett Browning

$\mathcal{T}$ell her how terrific
she's looking.

∾

$\mathcal{S}$urprise her with a box of
Godiva chocolates.

∾

$\mathcal{P}$ut a love note in his
shaving kit before he leaves
on a business trip.

Young Love

The hardest thing to wait for
is your first kiss.   —Age 16

The sweetest sound of all is
that of my own name spoken
by a boy I care about.   —Age 18

Don't be afraid to love. You
have the memories forever.
                                                —Age 14

❧

*Frankie and Johnny were
lovers, my gawd, how they
could love,
Swore to be true to each other,
true as the stars above;
He was her man,
but he done her wrong.*

—Traditional ballad

*C*ompose your own special
toast to each other.

❧

*B*ring home her
favorite magazine.

❧

*R*espect each other's need
for privacy.

*T*o love and
be loved is the
greatest joy in
the world.

A man may be said to love
most truly that woman in
whose company he can feel
drowsy in comfort.

—George Jean Nathan

❧

The love that we have
in our youth is superficial
compared to the love
that an old man has for
his wife.

—Will Durant

*And hand in hand, on
the edge of the sand,
They danced by the light
of the moon,
The moon,
The moon,
They danced by the light
of the moon.*

—Edward Lear

I've learned that . . .

you know you're in love
when the same person who
makes you *so* happy can
make you *so* mad. —Age 21

you should never spend a lot
of money on the first date.

—Age 19

I have spread my dreams
under your feet;
Tread softly because you
tread on my dreams.

—William Butler Yeats

∾

*U*nable are the Loved to die
For Love is immortality.

—Emily Dickinson

Love is of all passions
the strongest, for it attacks
simultaneously the head,
the heart, and the senses.

—Voltaire

❧

A person in love mistakes a
pimple for a dimple.

$\mathscr{P}$erfect love casts out fear.

—1 John 4:18

❧

$\mathscr{I}$t is best to love wisely, no
doubt; but to love foolishly is
better than not to be able to
love at all.

—William Makepeace Thackeray

$\mathcal{I}$ve learned that . . .

the best weight-loss program
is a broken heart. —Age 23

one of the greatest gifts my
parents gave me was their
love for each other. —Age 16

Shut up

and

kiss me.

—Mary Chapin Carpenter

$\mathcal{W}$hat appears at first sight extremely heavy, love will make most light.

—Christopher Harvey

∞

$\mathcal{L}$*ove is like an hourglass, with the heart filling up as the brain empties.*

—Jules Renard

*And then I asked him
with my eyes to ask again
yes and then he asked me
would I yes . . . and his
heart was going like mad
and yes I said
yes I will Yes.*

—James Joyce

The heart that loves is forever young.

—Greek proverb

❧

Man's love is of man's life a thing apart; 'Tis woman's whole existence.

—Lord Byron

*T*ake good care
of those
you love.

*I*t's impossible to love
and be wise.

—Francis Bacon

❧

*L*ove gives us in a moment
what we can hardly attain by
effort after years of toil.

—Goethe

The magic of first love is our ignorance that it can ever end.

—Benjamin Disraeli

∾

A man falls in love through his eyes, a woman through her ears.

—Woodrow Wyatt

I ne'er was struck before
   that hour
With love so sudden and
   so sweet,
Her face it bloomed like
   a sweet flower
And stole my heart away
   complete.

—John Clare

                  ❧

That Love is all there is,

Is all we know of Love.

—Emily Dickinson

$\mathcal{I}$'ve learned that . . .

once a relationship is over,
if you experienced more
smiles than tears, then it
wasn't a waste of time.

—Age 26

listening to sad country
songs is the last thing you
should do after a breakup.

—Age 24

You are always new. The last of your kisses was even the sweetest; the last smile the brightest; the last movement the gracefullest.

—John Keats

Young Love

When you like a boy, all you
do is wonder if he likes you.
Then he asks you out, and
all you do is wonder if he
will break up with you.

—Age 15

If you kiss someone on the
back of the neck, it spreads.

—Age 16

If ever two were one,
then surely we.
If ever man were loved by
wife, then thee.

—Anne Bradstreet

∽

A woman unsatisfied must
have luxuries. But a
woman who loves a man
would sleep on a board.

—D. H. Lawrence

The mistake we make is
when we seek to be loved,
instead of loving.
What makes us cowardly is
the fear of losing that love.

—Charlotte Yonge

∞

*Love comforteth like
sunshine after rain.*

—William Shakespeare

$\mathcal{I}$'ve learned that . . .

you know you're in love
when you want to tell
everyone about it, even
though they haven't asked.

—Age 27

just because he says he'll
call you doesn't mean he
will.
                    —Age 20

In the degree that we love will we be loved.

—Ralph Waldo Trine

∞

Love is friendship set on fire.

—Jeremy Taylor

∞

An old man in love is like a flower in winter.

—Old proverb

There is nothing holier,
   in this life of ours,
than the first consciousness
   of love—
the first fluttering of its
   silken wings.

—Henry Wadsworth Longfellow

❧

How much better is your
      love than wine.

—Song of Solomon 4:10

*L*ove suddenly
makes everything
seem possible.

$\mathcal{S}$low dance.

❧

$\mathcal{M}$ake your anniversary
an all-day event.

❧

$\mathcal{H}$old hands in the movies.

*L*ove is the only gold.

—Alfred, Lord Tennyson

☙

*If you have it, you don't
need to have anything
else, and if you don't have
it, it doesn't much matter
what else you have.*

—Sir James M. Barrie

An archeologist is the
best husband any woman can
have: the older she
gets, the more interested
he is in her.

—Agatha Christie

∽

*I'll think of another way
to get him back. After all,
tomorrow is another day.*

—Scarlett O'Hara

$\mathcal{I}$'ve learned that . . .

I love to open my eyes when my husband is kissing me so that I can see his eyes closed while he is kissing me.

—Age 31

the older I get the more pretty girls I remember kissing as a young man.

—Age 84

The way to love anything
is to realize it might
be lost.

—G. K. Chesterton

✺

And stand together yet not
too near together:
For the pillars of the temple
stand apart,
And the oak tree and cypress
grow not in each other's
shadow.

—Kahlil Gibran

$\mathcal{D}$rink to me only with
thine eyes,
And I will pledge with
mine;
And leave a kiss but
in the cup,
And I'll not look for wine.

—Ben Jonson

*T*o explain a romantic
breakup, simply say,
"It was all my fault."

❧

*L*augh at her jokes.

❧

*W*atch his favorite TV program
with him—even if you don't
like it.

Love is like the measles;
all the worse when it
comes late.

—Douglas Jerrold

'Tis better to have loved
and lost
Than never to have loved
at all.

—Alfred, Lord Tennyson

$\mathcal{I}$ve learned that . . .

it doesn't matter how your
husband squeezes the
toothpaste; the important
thing is how he squeezes
you.　　　　　—Age 54

you can't get through life
without a girlfriend.

　　　　　　　　　　—Age 9

∽

$\mathcal{L}$ife is slippery.
We all need
a loving hand
to hold on to.

*I'll tell you something
I think you'll
     understand,
Then I'll say that
     something,
I want to hold your hand.*

—John Lennon
and Paul McCartney

*There is no surprise
more magical than the
surprise of being loved;
it is God's finger on
man's shoulder.*

—Charles Morgan

*A*fter a misunderstanding,
be the first to say,
"I'm sorry."

❧

*W*hen someone tells you,
"I love you," never say,
"No you don't."

❧

*E*ven when you're angry, treat
each other with respect.

Young Love

A kiss on the beach when there is a full moon is the closest thing to heaven.

—Age 16

A girl can fall in and out of love in a hurry.

—Age 15

Love reckons hours for months, and days for years; and every little absence is an age.

—John Dryden

Let no one who loves be called altogether unhappy. Even love unreturned has its rainbow.

—James M. Barrie

$\mathcal{N}$ever give an anniversary
gift that has to be plugged in.

❧

$\mathcal{D}$evelop a hobby you
both enjoy.

❧

$\mathcal{T}$ake dance lessons together.

$\mathscr{I}$'ve learned that . . .

everything sounds romantic
in a foreign language, no
matter what is said. —Age 27

a woman never gets too old
not to want to be held in a
man's arms. —Age 68

Send her flowers
where she works.

∾

Spend time with
other happy couples.

∾

Take some silly photos of
the two of you in an
instant-photo booth.

Buy her a cuddly teddy bear.

❧

The sound of a kiss is
not so loud as that of a
cannon, but its echo lasts a
great deal longer.

—Oliver Wendell Holmes

$\mathcal{L}$et your sweetheart overhear your saying wonderful things about her.

☙

$\mathcal{R}$egardless of how angry you are, never sleep apart.

☙

$\mathcal{P}$ray together.

Assure your partner that
you're committed to her and
will always be there when
she needs you.

∾

What is love? . . .
It is the morning and
the evening star.

—Sinclair Lewis

*Two souls with but
a single thought,
Two hearts that beat
as one.*

—Von Munch Bellinghausen

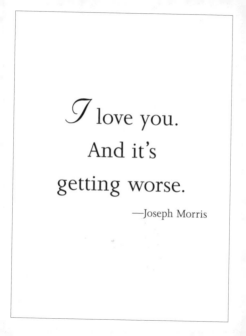

$\mathscr{I}$ love you.
And it's
getting worse.

—Joseph Morris

Call when you're going
to be late.

❧

Memorize her favorite
love poem.

❧

Keep your promises.

Love doesn't sit there
like a stone. *It* has to be
made like bread;
remade all the time,
made new.

—Ursula K. Le Guin

☙

All mankind loves a lover.

—Ralph Waldo Emerson

The realities of life bind us,
but love, great love,
introduces us to a universe of
unlimited possibilities.

❧

My life has been
awaiting you,
Your footfall was my
own heart's beat.

—Paul Cavafy

To love is to admire with
the heart; to admire is to
love with the mind.

—Theophile Gantier

❧

I love you,
not only for what you are,
But for what I am
when I am with you.

—Roy Croft

$\mathcal{I}$'ve learned that . . .

love will break your heart,
but it's worth it.   —Age 26

a kiss isn't a kiss without a
smack.   —Age 64

when you're in love, it
shows.   —Age 28

∾

$We\ two$

form a multitude.

—Ovid

❧

She was a child and I was a
    child,
In this kingdom by the sea,
But we loved with a love that
    was more than love—
I and my Annabel Lee.

—Edgar Allan Poe

*It's curious how,
when you're in love,
you yearn to go about
doing acts of kindness
to everybody.*

—P. G. Wodehouse

❧

The first duty of love
is to listen.

—Paul Tillich

There is a lady sweet
   and kind,
Was never a face so pleased
   my mind;
I did but see her passing by,
And yet I love her till
   I die.

                              —Anonymous

Young Love

I would rather have a best friend than a boyfriend, except maybe on a Friday night. —Age 20

My mom is always right about my boyfriends.

—Age 22

$\mathcal{D}$on't be critical of each other's friends.

❧

$\mathcal{N}$ever discuss past loves.

❧

$\mathcal{R}$ead Men Are from Mars, Women Are from Venus by John Gray (HarperCollins).

*H*ow bold
one gets when
one is sure
of being loved!

—Sigmund Freud

$\mathcal{B}$uy a little heart-shaped pillow and put it where she can see it every night before she goes to sleep.

❧

$\mathcal{S}$hare a banana split.

❧

$\mathcal{G}$ive each other big hugs at least twice a day.

$\mathcal{D}$inah doesn't
Treat him right
But if he'd
Shave,
Dyna-mite!
Burma-Shave

—Advertising Road Sign

In literature as in love,

we are astonished at what

is chosen by others.

—Andre Maurois

❧

*L*ove is the triumph of
imagination over
intelligence.

—H. L. Mencken

*Two such as you with such
    a master speed
Cannot be parted nor be
    swept away
From one another once you
    are agreed
That life is only life
    forevermore
Together wing to wing and
    oar to oar.*

—Robert Frost

*P*hone your sweetheart just
to say "I love you."

❧

*R*emind him,
"Drive safely,
I love you."

❧

*G*ive back rubs without
being asked.

Sarah, my love for you is deathless. . . . If I do not return, my dear Sarah, never forget how much I loved you nor that when my last breath escapes me on the battlefield it will whisper your name.

—Maj. Sullivan Ballou,
one week prior to his death at
the First Battle of Bull Run

*L*ove and a cough cannot
be hid.
—George Herbert

❧

A kiss is a lovely trick
designed by nature to stop
speech when words become
superfluous.
—Ingrid Bergman

I've learned that . . .

you know your husband still loves you when there are two brownies left and he takes the smaller one. —Age 39

after all these years, I still have a crush on my husband.

—Age 38

*M*arry only
for love.

*L*ove like ours can
never die.

—Rudyard Kipling

❧

*A*bsence is to love as wind
is to fire;
*I*t extinguishes the small
and kindles the great.

—Roger de Bussy-Rabutin

*Love is what
you've been through
with somebody.*

—James Thorten

∽

*Those who love deeply
never grow old;
they may die of old age,
but they die young.*

—Sir Arthur Wing Pinero

$\mathcal{S}$hare your dreams.

✍

$\mathcal{B}$ecome each other's
best friend.

Forgive quickly.

∾

Kiss slowly.

*L*ove conquers
all things;
let us too
surrender to
Love.

—Virgil